P9-DGH-854

**PRESENTED TO**

Jason and Colleen Warren

**FROM**

The FCA Staff

Christmas '99

**DATE**

# A *Champion's* HEART

## Qualities for Success in Life and Sports

# Jim Sheard, Ph.D.
# James F. Gauss, Ph.D.

Project Editor: Pat Matuszak

Designed by Koechel Peterson & Associates, Minneapolis, Minnesota

ISBN: 08499-5527-0

Printed in the USA

# CONTENTS

# INTRODUCTION

## THE APOSTLE PAUL WRITES:

*Do you not know that those who run in a race
all run, but one receives the prize?
Run in such a way that you may obtain it.
And everyone who competes for the prize
is temperate in all things.
Now they do it to obtain a perishable crown,
but we for an imperishable crown.
Therefore I run thus: not with uncertainty.
Thus I fight: not as one who beats the air.
But I discipline my body and bring it into
subjection, lest, when I have preached to others,
I myself should become disqualified.*

1 CORINTHIANS 9:24-27

Paul understood what it means to have a champion's heart. To excel we must exercise self-control. We cannot be aimless in our focus. Instead we direct our total effort on the imperishable crown, eternal life in Christ. Our reward is in our relationship with Him, both here on earth and in heaven.

A champion's heart is one that is being molded into a likeness of the heart of Christ. By learning about Him, and committing our heart to Him, we grow into His likeness. Our relationship with Him produces a renewing of our character as God develops in us the qualities essential for true success. The wisdom we gain from the Bible, along with the guidance of others, helps us grow in commitment, character, and competence. This is how we can have a champion's heart.

JIM SHEARD & JAMES F. GAUSS,
*July 1999*

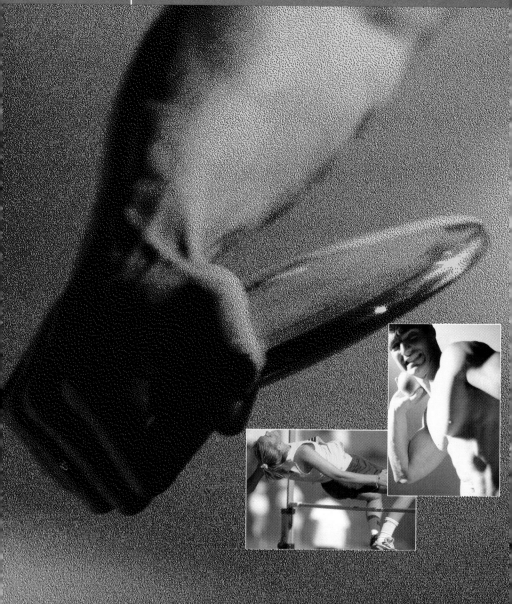

**Chapter 1** | **Coachable in Attitude**

Where there is no
counsel [coaching],
the people fall;
But in the multitude of
counselors [coaches]
there is safety.

Proverbs 15:22

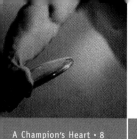

# SUCCESS IN ATHLETICS REQUIRES A COACHABLE SPIRIT OR ATTITUDE.

We cannot achieve our full potential on our own. We must all be willing to listen to and learn from the advice of those with more experience and knowledge. In all walks of life there are those with the insight to observe our performance, identify our potential, and improve our skills.

*You* can tell a lot about a player
by how he interacts with the coach . . .
a player who listens to the coach,
tries to do what he's told,
and keeps lines of communication
open is a bonus for any team.

KEN RUETTGER
*Offensive Line with Green Bay Packers for ten Years*

A coachable attitude is important for achievement and success in every aspect of life. On our first
job, and at every phase of our career, there are people who can give us the feedback we need for growth
and improvement. They may be higher in the organization, coworkers, those who report to us, or train-
ers. Successful people in all walks of life have
learned to be receptive to feedback and instruction.
They are teachable and coachable. In short, they are
good listeners. They listen to people around them,
and they learn from what they hear. They seek out,
and listen to, many sources. After considering many
different perspectives they focus their attention on
the wisest counsel.

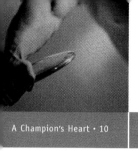

# THE IMPORTANCE OF ATTITUDE

College and Olympic-bound athletes find the best coaches to help them develop and fine-tune their potential. Professional and amateur golfers seek coaching in the physical and mental skills of this demanding and frustrating sport. Professional athletes in team sports like baseball, football, basketball, hockey, and soccer were coached from their youth in how to contribute to the team effort. They must continue throughout their career to learn how to block and tackle, turn the double play, or double-team an opponent. They must learn to excel at their position from specialized coaches. They are still being coached as they prepare for the league championship, Super Bowl, World Series, World Cup, or Olympics. We never achieve a status where we no longer need a coach.

Even professional athletes at the level of Michael Jordan, Tiger Woods, Wayne Gretzky, and Betsy King seek the advice of their coaches. Surely, we too need coaching, whether it is in athletics, work, or spiritual growth. Regardless of our skills, status, or accomplishments, we must listen to feedback in order to be successful and to achieve our full potential. There will always be people available to us with insights to help us grow in our work, hobbies, studies, and

*However, when He, the Spirit of truth,*

*has come, He will guide you into all truth;*

*for He will not speak on His own authority,*

*but whatever He hears He will speak;*

*and He will tell you things to come.*

*He will glorify Me, for He will take of what is Mine*

*and declare it to you.*

JOHN 16:13-14

athletics. Lou Holtz, Head Football Coach at the University of South Carolina explains how a coach-able attitude helps athletes this way: "The *attitude* you choose to assume toward life and everything it brings you will determine whether you realize your aspirations. Your *talent* determines what you can do. Your *motivation* determines how much you are willing to do. Your *attitude* determines how well you do it."

It is the word of God in the Bible, along with the direction of the Holy Spirit, which serves as our fore-most source of advice. God's purpose and direction for our life are revealed to us as we seek to grow in a relationship with Jesus Christ. His direction is made clear through His word and the guidance of the Holy Spirit. He also provides wise teachers to help us walk along that path.

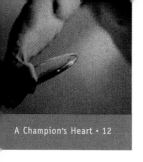

The psalmist says, *"Your testimonies also are my delight and my counselors"* (Psalm 119:24). In verses 98 through 100 of this psalm, we are told that in learning and following God's wisdom we will be made wiser than our enemies, have more insight than all our teachers, and have more understanding than the elders. It is clear that God wants to teach us. He will give us incredible wisdom. He will make us wise beyond our own natural understanding if we seek His counsel and submit ourselves to being coached in life and faith by Him.

## CHOOSE YOUR ATTITUDE

*R*emember, you can't start over in life's marathon. You often can't choose your circumstance or situation, but you do have the privilege of choosing your attitude.

BOB BARDWELL
*Wheelchair Marathoner*

NHL hockey player Adam Burt asked his friend Bobby Holik, who skates for New Jersey, why they looked unstoppable in the finals against Detroit a couple of years earlier. Bobby said, "If we listen to our coach and follow his game plan, we win." His reflection applies to our life as spiritual athletes:

*If* I listen to God
and follow His game plan,
I'll win.

BOBBY HOLIK
*NHL Player*

Spiritual athletes seek God's counsel in every important matter of life. They surround themselves with wise and godly men and women who can help them achieve their full potential. To seek anything less than the very best counsel leads to under-achievement. It makes for less than complete development of our potential for growth and fulfillment. To decide we no longer need coaching in some aspect of our life is to choose an attitude that is doomed to underachievement and ultimately to failure.

*I* try to spend time each day in prayer or meditation.

I also spend time in the Scriptures each day.

My time spent in this fashion has been a

real source of strength to me.

In the book of Isaiah, it says that "those who

wait upon the Lord will renew their strength.

They will mount up with wings like eagles.

They will run and not grow weary,

they will walk and not faint."

I know that God . . . provides the necessary

strength to those who desire to serve Him.

TOM OSBORNE
*Former Head Football Coach — University of Nebraska*

Another former head football coach, Tom Landry, also comments on what it means to apply the teachings of Christ in our everyday life. He says that one of the results of seeking to follow after Christ is that we should take on some of the character qualities of Christ. We should begin to grow in qualities like integrity and patience. He says that this is the essence of what it means to be a Christian. But Coach Landry says it does not end there. In addition to providing us with a character model, "Faith frees a person to do his best to achieve his potential." That is what it is like to have a coach who really cares about us. The coach wants us to achieve our potential. It also helps if we have a coachable attitude so that we seek out his wisdom and listen to his guidance.

God wants us to have faith in Him so that we can be free to become all that He intended. It will require a coachable attitude on our part.

**POWER** point #1

God is our #1 coach. Seek His counsel and that of other coaches.

And whatever you do in word or deed, do all in the name of the Lord Jesus, giving thanks to God the Father through Him.

Colossians 3:17

## OUR PERSPECTIVE GREATLY INFLUENCES HOW WE THINK AND PERFORM.

To succeed in athletics, or any other challenge, we must maintain a positive perspective. No matter what the obstacle or opposition, successful people believe that they can overcome and win the battle. It is no wonder Henry Ford has often been quoted saying, "Whether you think you can, or whether you think you can't, you're right." The Scriptures present this same idea: *"For as he thinks in his heart, so is he"* (Proverbs 23:7a).

*W*hen you've got God in your life, it's so much easier
to deal with a lot of the pressures and situations
because when the demands come down on you,
it's so easy to just pray about it
and let God worry about it.

JEFF GORDON
*NASCAR Driver*

$\mathscr{E}$verybody out here [on the Ladies Professional Golf Tour] can play.
The ones who stay mentally positive and who can
see themselves winning are the ones who
who are going to be successful.
Those are the golfers who are going to play
the best golf year after year.

BARB MUCHA
*LPGA Tour Player*

Our mindset influences our performance and there is no substitute for a positive outlook. We need to be positive about our own skills, opportunities, teammates, and leaders. We need to think and speak positively about the organizations, products and services, and people we represent. Without such a perspective, we are doomed before we even begin. Understandably, it is especially hard to have a positive perspective in the face of adversity and personal doubt. For many people this requires a significant adjustment. Even when they start with a positive outlook, when the going gets rough, they may give up on themselves or others. We must find ways to overcome this very human tendency.

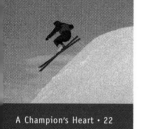

Successful athletes and coaches do not go into a competition expecting to lose. Even if they thought of the possibility, they would not express it openly, or dwell on such a thought pattern. While their opponent might appear bigger, more experienced, more skilled, better coached, and have a better record, the successful athlete and coach look for ways to utilize their strengths. They also shore up their limitations and seek the strategy that can produce a victory.

*C*hrist has given me authority over fear. I can pray it away because my focus is on Jesus Christ, not on riding bulls.

CODY MARK CUSTER
*1992 World Champion Rodeo Bull Rider*

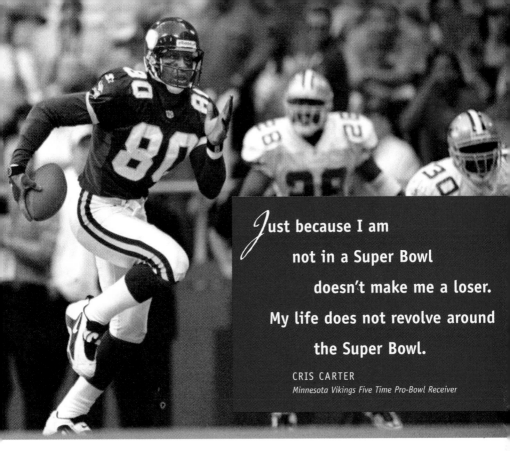

*J*ust because I am
not in a Super Bowl
doesn't make me a loser.
My life does not revolve around
the Super Bowl.

CRIS CARTER
*Minnesota Vikings Five Time Pro-Bowl Receiver*

Developing a positive perspective in life and sports involves clarifying the goal and the reason for the competition. The best athletes and coaches realize that success is defined by much more than win/loss records, statistics, and fan appeal. Long-term success and significance lie in the human spirit and in fulfillment of God-given talent. It is easier to be positive when we understand the meaning and purpose of life. It also helps to have realistic expectations. When we understand the character-building process we are going through, we are better able to deal with both the successes and the setbacks.

In our life of faith, we must also look beyond the circumstances. Our faith in God and in his Son, Jesus Christ, gives us an eternal hope. It is the ultimate positive perspective. God expects us, with the eyes of faith, to see beyond our circumstances, the obstacles, and the winter of our discontent. He expects us to see ourselves and others in a brand new way: loved, precious, created for a purpose, and victorious through His victory on the cross. In return, all He asks is that we give thanks and acknowledge Him as Creator and Lord.

*I* believe that if you
yield your life to God,
and seek to know Him better,
then He will give you
a proper perspective on life.

TOM OSBORNE
*Former Head Football Coach,*
*University of Nebraska*

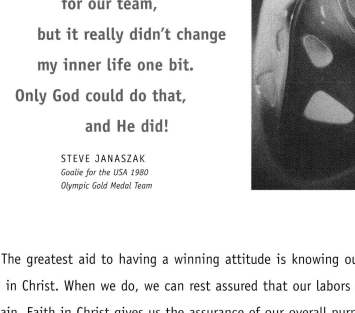

$\mathscr{T}$he Olympic medal was an
outstanding accomplishment
for our team,
but it really didn't change
my inner life one bit.
Only God could do that,
and He did!

STEVE JANASZAK
*Goalie for the USA 1980*
*Olympic Gold Medal Team*

The greatest aid to having a winning attitude is knowing our position in Christ. When we do, we can rest assured that our labors are not in vain. Faith in Christ gives us the assurance of our overall purpose for living. It gives us confidence that the Creator cares about our well being. Out of that assurance we can seek to carry our winning, positive perspective into all we do. Remember that by having a winning attitude we can still be a gracious winner or loser. Regardless of the outcome on the field of play, in the long run we will know that our efforts are not in vain. By adhering to the "Coach's" winning game plan for life, presented for us in the Bible, we can rest assured that we will finish the race with the crown of His glory.

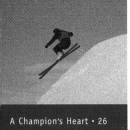

*Therefore, my beloved brethren, be steadfast,*
*immovable, always abounding in the work of the Lord,*
*knowing that your labor is not in vain in the Lord.*

1 CORINTHIANS 15:58

## THE BEST PLAN FOR MY LIFE

*I* know that God has the ultimate plan—the best plan
for my life. Obviously, I can't float through life and
let it all happen. I have to try my hardest, and I also
have to give thanks to Him for giving me this talent.
And I have to accept whatever happens, because I
know in the end, as long as I'm giving 100 percent
and trying my hardest, that's the right thing.

LOREN ROBERTS
*PGA Tour Player*

*W*hen I invited Christ into my heart,

I began depending on God's strength,

love, and power during the

most important moments in my life—

As it came time for the final penalty kick

[in the 1994 World Cup finals]—

It was then that I understood

how important it is not to be alone.

God never left my side.

CLAUDIO TAFFAREL
*Goalkeeper, 1994 World Cup Champion Brazilian Soccer Team*

*I* try to live my life as if Jesus

was living inside of me.

I try to make choices

He would make.

MIKE EAGLES
*Center for NHL Washington Capitals*

*T*alent is God-given.

**BE HUMBLE.**

Fame is man-given.

**BE THANKFUL.**

Conceit is self-given.

**BE CAREFUL.**

JOHN WOODEN
*Legendary UCLA Head Basketball Coach*

## A MAN OF FAITH

*I* want people to see me as a man of God.

I want my kids to see me as a man of God.

In fact, I want the fact

that I am a man of God

to be so overpowering

that they will forget that

I even played football.

REGGIE WHITE
*Green Bay Packers Pro-Bowl Defensive Lineman*

**POWER**point #2

The right perspective comes from having Jesus Christ at the center of our life.

| **Committed to Achievement**

Commit your works
to the LORD,
and your thoughts
will be established.

PROVERBS 16:3

# THE NEED FOR ACHIEVEMENT IS A PART OF HUMAN NATURE.

The environment and society in which we live also encourage it. However, God's perspective of winning and achievement is different from that of our society. For the spiritual athlete, winning and achievement involve setting goals in relationship to our own abilities and the obstacles to be overcome. Meeting goals relevant to our own abilities is more important than meeting a standard relevant to the abilities and opportunities of others.

*I*'m just a regular guy who happens

to do something pretty well.

Everybody does something well.

Everybody.

MARK MARTIN
*NASCAR Driver*

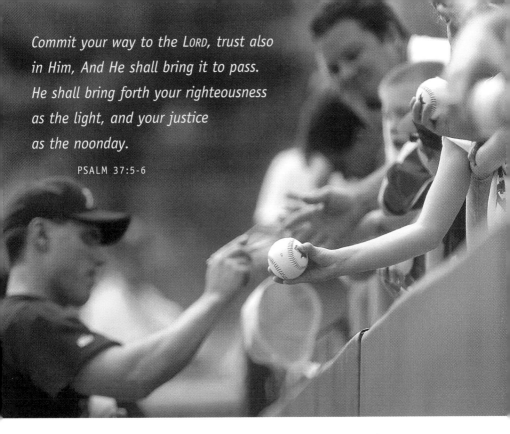

*Commit your way to the LORD, trust also in Him, And He shall bring it to pass. He shall bring forth your righteousness as the light, and your justice as the noonday.*

PSALM 37:5-6

Achievement should be measured by God's standards rather than standards dictated by society. The spiritual athlete is committed to fulfilling God's will for his or her life. Fulfillment is winning at the real issues of life. It is winning gradually, in incremental ways, and making a lasting difference in the lives of others. We gain fulfillment by committing to use our abilities for God's purposes. We have been created in the image of the almighty Father, the Creator of heaven and earth. He created us to achieve His purposes on earth and to reside with Him in heaven upon our death. By fulfilling God's plan, our achievements have lasting significance.

As spiritual athletes we are to seek to discover and fulfill God's purpose in our life. Since fulfillment is achievement that has lasting significance, it is not measured by awards and trophies. The person who finishes last in a marathon may have greater fulfillment than the person who wins the race. The winner may have had a relatively poor race for his or her capabilities, while the person who finished last may have had a personal best. Ultimately, we seek to serve God and fulfill the potential He provides through our abilities, gifts, and opportunities.

## WINNERS

The last wheel chair marathoner to finish
enhanced my definition of winning.
Besides first place winners, there are second-,
third-, and fourth-place winners.
The winners that day were those who
(1)did their best,
(2) didn't quit and
(3) delighted in finishing.

BOB BARDWELL

Commitment to achievement involves utilizing our unique God-given talents. God wants us to find fulfillment when we rely on Him to face challenges and opportunities. Therefore, it is important to set goals that stretch and challenge our unique abilities. When we do so we allow God to be in control of the gifts He has given to us. He also helps us to overcome our limitations so that these achievements become realistic in spite of the obstacles that come our way.

*You* just do the best job you can.

You work hard on and off the race track,

and I think good things come

to people who dedicate their

lives to it and work hard at it.

JEFF GORDON
*NASCAR Driver*

*Do you see a man who excels in his work?*

*He will stand before kings;*

*He will not stand before unknown men.*

PROVERBS 22:29

Our achievements in athletics, work, and life are often visible and measured. For example, achievement in athletics can often be boiled down to win-loss records, championships, times, and distances. Measurements from stop watches, tape measures, videotapes, and scores of games or matches can be recorded and observed. Even when there are disputed calls by referees or judges, the measurements and record books speak for themselves.

**Perfection is what you are striving for,**

**but perfection is an impossibility.**

**However, striving for perfection**

**is not an impossibility.**

JOHN WOODEN
*Legendary UCLA Head Basketball Coach*

In life we attempt to measure our achievements in a variety of ways. Companies and organizations measure their achievements by sales, profits, growth, and improvement relative to the competition. Unfortunately, individuals usually measure their achievements in terms of income, advancement in the organization, personal growth, and by what they have been able to acquire with their money. Some of the other goals in life are much harder to quantify, but are also extremely important. They include our time with family, our relationships, our service to others, and our growth in character.

*E*very day I go out and enjoy what I do.

God has given me a great talent

to play baseball.

So many times we

take things for granted.

I know I've worked as hard as I can

and it's because of Jesus Christ.

JOE CARTER
*7 seasons with the World Champion Toronto Blue Jays,
then the Baltimore Orioles*

## MY VERY BEST—FOR HIM

*I* feel that God gave me the talent

and the strength to maintain

a career in hockey.

As a Christian, whatever I do

should be my

very best—for Him.

DOUG JARVIS
*Retired from the NHL in '87 after 13 years — The National Hockey
League's "Iron Man" with a record 964 consecutive games.*

Our achievements as spiritual athletes are not readily measurable. They are referred to in Scripture as "fruits," and they are often not readily seen and can seldom be measured. The fruits of our commitment to serving the Lord come about, not so much by our pain and toil, but by the commitment of our heart to the Lord. They are the result of abiding in Him. Fruit is the product of turning our efforts and heart over to Him. It includes the impact we have on those around us. It is the help we give in the name of the Lord to those in need. It is the encouragement found in our spoken or unspoken gesture of love. Fruit is also the result of our prayers and concerns for those in our home and far away in other countries. The only way to bear fruit is through the Spirit of Jesus working in us. It is achieved in proportion to our commitment to achieving His will through our life.

# A CLEAR GOAL IN MIND

*The* quality of a man's life

is in direct proportion

to his commitment

to excellence.

TOM LANDRY

While that is a rather broad statement covering the spectrum of a person's life, it can be broken down into more specific commitments to achievement. For example, Mr. Landry points out that it means that we need to start each day with a clear goal in mind. We have to say to ourselves that we will do our best in every area of life. We will give our total effort to the cause and not choose the easy route.

# POWER point #3

Talent comes from God. Commitment is a choice we make. Achievement comes from commitment to God.

# Chapter 4

# Driven by Purpose

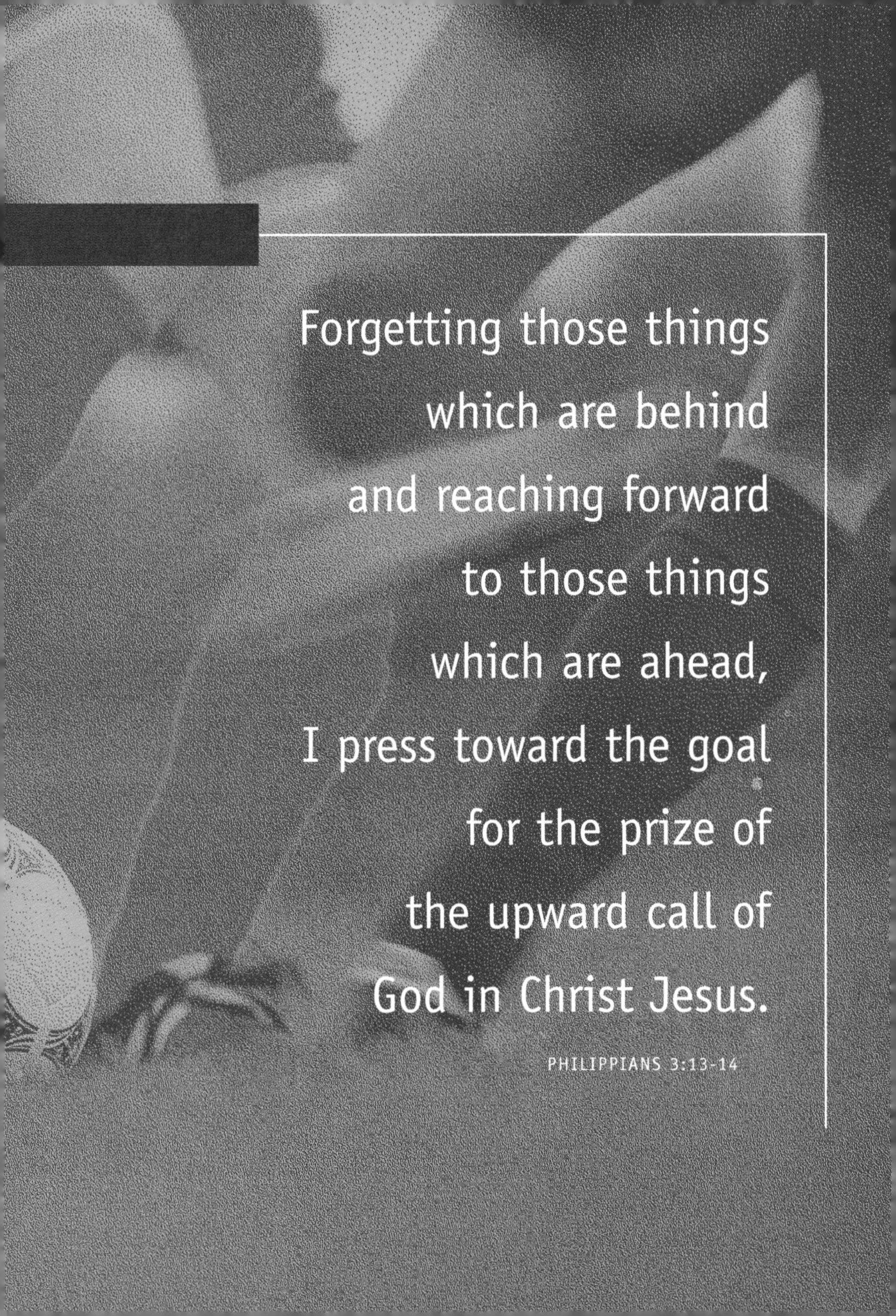

Forgetting those things
which are behind
and reaching forward
to those things
which are ahead,
I press toward the goal
for the prize of
the upward call of
God in Christ Jesus.

PHILIPPIANS 3:13-14

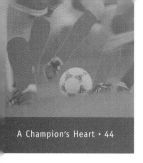

If our only purpose in athletics is to win and become the champion, there will be disappointment and frustration. Likewise, if we focus on material gain and worldly accomplishment throughout our life, it will be an empty and endless quest. On the other hand, when we focus on the upward call of Christ Jesus our purpose is clear. By focusing our attention on the person of Jesus and aligning ourselves with Him and His word, we are driven by a worthy purpose. There is a renewing of our mind into the image of Christ Jesus. Our character becomes more and more like His.

*The* **purpose of life is to be found through having Christ in your life, understanding what His plan is, and following that plan.**

JULIUS IRVING ("DR. J")
*ABA and then NBA Player with the Philadelphia 76ers*

*You* don't really know how
strongly you feel about something
until you have had to stand up for it.

DARRELL WALTRIP
*NASCAR Driver*

A sense of purpose for life comes from knowing
Christ as our Lord and Savior. By knowing Him and
having a relationship with Him, we want to do His
will. We will also be assured that our effort is not in
vain. It will be a powerful force, a sense of purpose,
so strong that we will strive to: *be steadfast,*
*immovable, always abounding in the work of the Lord,*
*knowing that your labor is not in vain in the Lord*
(1 Corinthians 15:58).

To be steadfast and immovable means to be
secure, certain, fixed, and unwavering. We need to
allow God, by faith in his word, to give us security
and certainty that he is who he says he is. We can
be assured that he will do what He says He will do.
This steadfast position will cause us to want to get
to know and serve Him better. It will cause us to be
driven with passion and purpose.

*P*hysical strength comes from training,

lifting one more weight. Or in the case

of a gymnast, doing one more flip.

But real courage and real strength comes from God.

MARY LOU RETTON
*Olympic Gold Medalist*

In sports, work, hobbies, and relationships, we need to be driven by our purpose. If Jesus is our ultimate purpose, and our security, the remaining issues in life become much clearer. We seek to achieve those things that will be honoring to our King. We strive to serve as His ambassadors. We are driven by a purpose that is beyond anything else we could ever hope to achieve.

As a follower of Christ, achievement in sports, development of talent as an athlete, and victory or defeat will be for His purposes and for the perfecting of our character. It is an overriding purpose that can drive us to levels beyond anything else we might have believed possible. It is also a purpose with meaning apart from any accomplishment or failure. We are driven to prepare for and "play the game" of life to the best of our God-given ability. There is glory in victory, even in defeat, if we have done our best with our abilities and if we have given the glory to God. This is contrary to our society's philosophy, which tends to overemphasize performance. Instead, we need to value what is inside people rather than how well they have performed a task.

*O*ur worth comes from who we are,
and not from what we do.

DAVE DRAVECKY
*Star pitcher for the San Francisco Giants*
*who lost his pitching arm to cancer.*

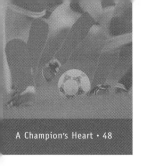

We need to refrain from having the point of view that God will help Christian athletes perform better than those who do not have a personal faith in Christ. We will not run faster, jump higher, or score more points because of our faith. But, as Coach Landry has pointed out, "a personal faith in God can change and improve anyone's character." Our faith in Christ can be an advantage to us as an athlete, student, teacher, parent, executive, or whatever occupation we are pursuing. It is our character that is most important in God's eyes.

*My* faith has helped me believe
there is always something better out there.
God has given me the ability
to be athletically competitive.
It's great to go out there and use it.

TONY PEREZ
*National Champion High School Wrestler*

*S*erving the Lord is the
central point of everything I do.

DAVID ROBINSON
*San Antonio Spurs Center and*
*NBA Most Valuable Player*

# THE DESIRE OF YOUR HEART

*Delight yourself also in the L*ORD*, and He shall give you the desires of your heart.*

PSALM 37:4

*I* keep [Psalm 37:4] in mind and put [it] on my golf balls because it always gives me an inner peace. It always reminds me that the Lord is with me at all times, regardless of whether I'm winning, regardless of whether I'm playing well or not. It always gives me peace. And if you have that peace, you're able to play to a level of ability you wouldn't believe.

DEWITT WEAVER
*PGA Senior Tour Player*

*I*'m sold out for God. There's nothing phony about this. I'm sold out. And it can't be any other way.

RANDALL CUNNINGHAM
*Vikings Pro-Bowl Quarterback*

# POWER point #4

**We will have the strength we need when God is the driving purpose for our life.**

| **Focused on Goals**

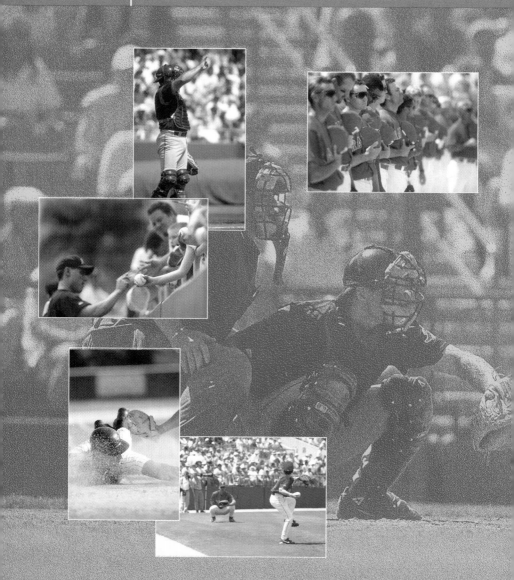

A man's heart
plans his way,
but the LORD
directs his steps.

PROVERBS 16:9

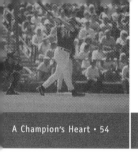

# GOALS FOCUS OUR EFFORTS

Goals help us to focus our effort. They help us to maintain a proper perspective and not to lose sight of the overall purpose.

**SHORT-TERM** (or immediate) goals in athletics may include focusing on the end zone, the strike zone, the hoop, the net, or the pin on the green. It could be running the first quarter of a mile run under a certain time, finishing a marathon, or getting the first serve in the service court. Short-term goals also apply to things like getting the lawn mowed before the weekend, being home with our family by dinnertime four out of five evenings this week, or completing a key project at work by Wednesday.

**INTERMEDIATE** goals may focus on the results we are seeking in a game or in a season. The goal could be to get a golf handicap to single digits, to qualify for a marathon, or make a high school varsity team. Examples outside of athletics include finishing a degree, taking a specialized training program, having the house painted by the Fourth of July, or taking our family on a memorable vacation.

Charlotte Smith set some goals for her basketball career:

## "I want to win the world championship and become the first woman to dunk on the professional level."

After basketball, Charlotte is interested in going into social work. She enjoys speaking to kids:

## "I try to speak about the importance of education and setting goals, and the importance of God."

CHARLOTTE SMITH
*Women's American Basketball League Player*

**LONG-TERM** goals are usually more significant and may take years to accomplish. For the gifted athlete, it may be getting a Division I athletic scholarship or winning an Olympic medal. Long-term goals may be more modest, but still very important. For example, being fit enough to walk the golf course and carry a golf bag for 18 holes at age 60. Long-term goals also apply to all aspects of our life. Goals may be financial in nature, such as saving money from a summer job to pay college expenses. For someone in their later years it could be to have the financial resources to retire at age 65. Other goals may relate to work, family, recreation, health, etc.

*T*he goal I believe is important is the goal of making the most of your abilities. That goal is within your reach.

JOHN WOODEN
*Legendary UCLA Head Basketball Coach*

*If* I don't set goals, I just dilly-dally around
and I don't have anything to work for.
I definitely think I have a chance
to go on the LPGA Tour.
I just have to put a lot of work in
and a lot of practice.

AMBER AMSTUTZ
*Ohio State Women's Golf Team*

The spiritual athlete knows how to focus on short-term, intermediate, and long-term goals. It does little good to focus time and attention on the wrong goals. They need to be important and meaningful. The spiritual athlete is able to discern which goals will help achieve valuable purposes in life and sports. This can only come from having our hearts and eyes focused on seeking the Lord's will for our lives. That means putting Him first in all that we do. It also means that we rely on the Bible as our guide in making important decisions. We look for the general principles and the basic tenets revealed in it and then seek to live accordingly. Dave Dravecky says that the general principles he uses to shape the game plan for his life come the Bible. "I want to be faithful to God, my family, my friends, and my calling. I want to live with integrity and make the most of my talents and the opportunities I am afforded in life. I want to love God with all my heart, soul, mind, and strength, and to love my neighbor as myself."

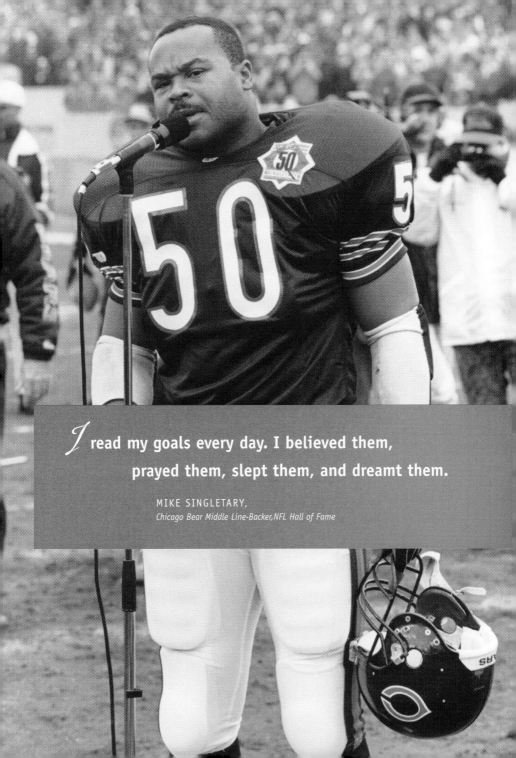

*I* read my goals every day. I believed them, prayed them, slept them, and dreamt them.

MIKE SINGLETARY,
*Chicago Bear Middle Line-Backer, NFL Hall of Fame*

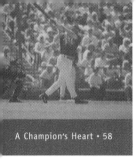

*I* want to be all the man of God
that Christ can enable me to be.

SCOTT FROST
*Quarterback for the Nebraska Cornhuskers
in 1996 and 1997*

*As for you, my son Solomon, know the God of your father,
and serve Him with a loyal heart and with a willing mind;
for the LORD searches all hearts and understands
all the intent of the thoughts.
If you seek Him, He will be found by you;
but if you forsake Him, He will cast you off forever.*

1 CHRONICLES 28:9-10

There are two key implications of this passage
from Chronicles. First, the Lord wants each of us to
build a temple for Him in our own heart. We are the
temple of the Holy Spirit and God wants us to be a
worthy temple through our thoughts and actions.
The second implication is that if we seek God with
our whole heart and a willing mind, He will show us
the goals that He wants us to fulfill for Him. He will
understand and help us with the plans and thoughts
we seek to accomplish.

Dave Johnson competed in the decathlon in the 1988, 1992, and 1996 Summer Olympics. Reebok spent millions of dollars on advertisements prior to the '92 Olympics in Barcelona setting up a rivalry between him and Dan O'Brien, both of the United States, for the title of the World's Greatest Athlete. It turned out that Dan did not make the U.S. team. Then, due to a cracked bone in his foot, Dave was fortunate even to compete and win the Bronze medal. He endured incredible pain to finish the ten-event competition. He described his experience:

"*I* ended up learning much more about life by not winning the gold. Don't get me wrong—I'm disappointed I didn't win, and I still struggle at times with anger at God for the way it happened. But the message from Him continues to come through that His loving purpose is being worked out in my life.... In the final analysis, reaching the goal or realizing the dream is not nearly as important as the person we've become along the way. Long after the thrill of victory or the agony of defeat has been faced, that person will endure. The more we allow ourselves to learn and grow in the process of reaching our goals, the better equipped we'll be to live a meaningful life and make a difference in the world."

DAVE JOHNSON

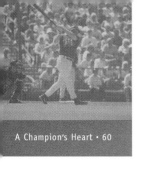

God uses the word *heart* to describe what is at the core of our purpose and focus in life. The heart is at the center of our will. God wants us to focus our hearts on Him and on the things He sees as important for our life. If we do, He will encourage us.

My son, if your heart is wise, my heart will rejoice—
indeed, I myself; yes, my inmost being will rejoice
when your lips speak right things.
Do not let your heart envy sinners,
but be zealous for the fear of the LORD all the day;
for surely there is a hereafter,
and your hope will not be cut off.
Hear, my son, and be wise;
And guide your heart in the way.

PROVERBS 23:15-19

The Scriptures also speak of the role of the eye in directing our path. This is not so much the physical eyes with which we see things around us, but the internal, spiritual eyes with which we see meaning, direction, and purpose for our life.

*The lamp of the body is the eye. Therefore, when your eye is good, your whole body also is full of light. But when your eye is bad, your body also is full of darkness. Therefore take heed that the light which is in you is not darkness.*

LUKE 11:34-35

*Let your eyes look straight ahead, and your eyelids look right before you.*

PROVERBS 4:25

There are far more good long-term goals than we can pursue. However, there are only a few worthy of our focus. When our heart is focused on the Lord and His will for our life, He will help us identify those goals worthy of our effort. Only God, and the wise counselors He places in our life, can help us determine the goals on which to focus. The spiritual athlete will continually seek the wisdom and direction of God to determine the highest priority goals and how to best accomplish them.

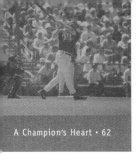

As Head Coach of the Dallas Cowboys, Tom Landry faced the uphill challenge of developing and inspiring his players after five losing seasons. In a letter to the players prior to the '65 training camp he defined the philosophy and goals for the team. He said there were three important principles that must be followed in the team effort to become winners:

"• **have a clear-cut objective**

• **recognize every resistance that will prevent you from reaching your objective**

• **have a plan of action that will overcome the resistances...**"

Mr. Landry made it clear to the team that the major objective was to win the championship. He said that objective could be broken down into minor objectives for each of the sources of resistance that had to be overcome. Demonstrating his attention to every possibility, Mr. Landry said that each of the minor objectives must be a major objective until it is attained. That gives some idea of why the Dallas Cowboys were to become "America's Team," the most successful football franchise for the next few years.

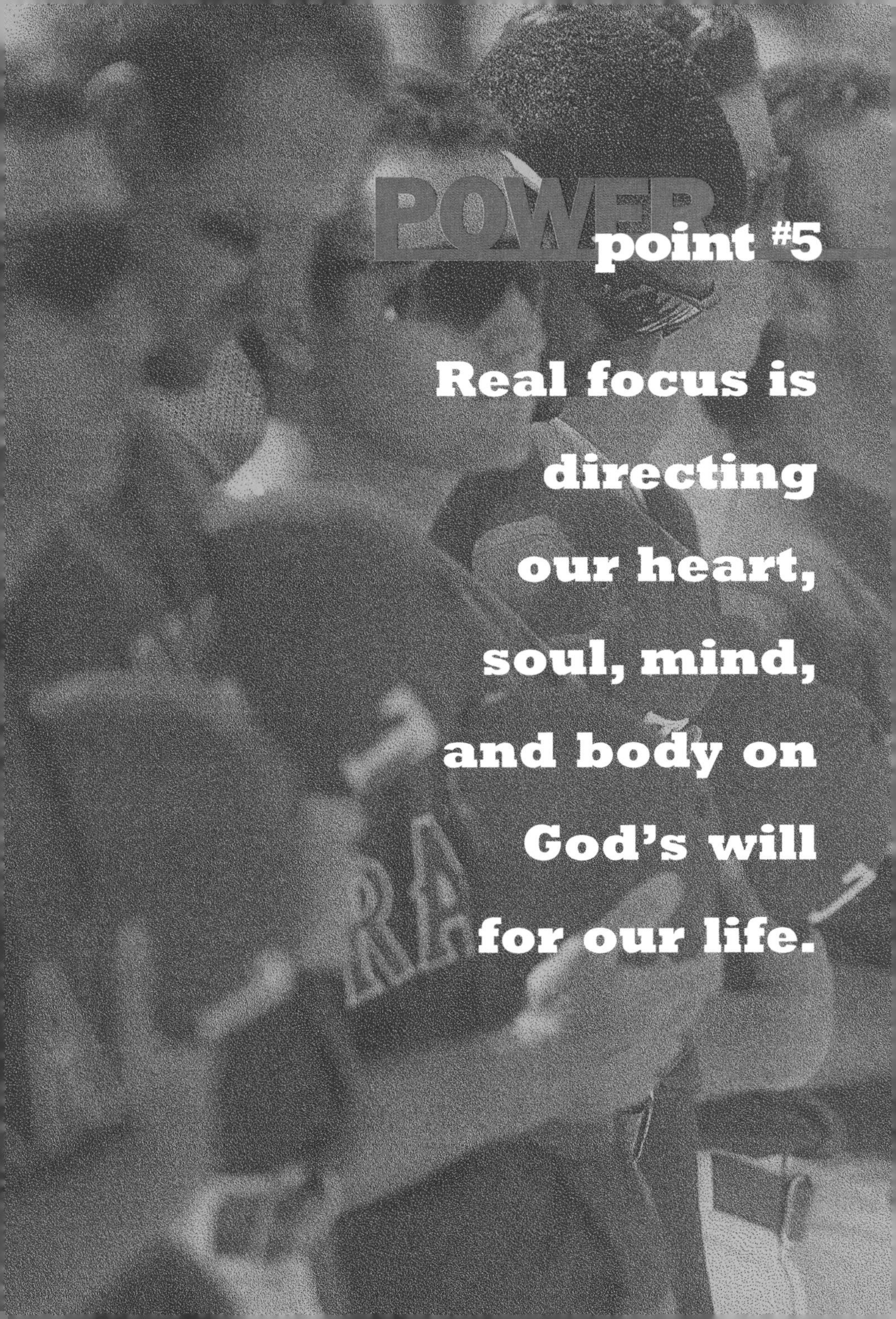

**POWER** point #5

Real focus is
directing
our heart,
soul, mind,
and body on
God's will
for our life.

Chapter 6 | **Disciplined in Effort**

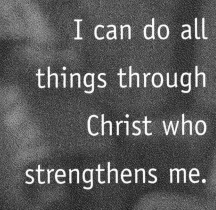

I can do all
things through
Christ who
strengthens me.

PHILIPPIANS 4:13

To prepare adequately for the challenges of competition, successful athletes follow a rigorous practice schedule on their own and with team members. They prepare their mind and body for the requirements of their sport and the demands of competition. In addition to the talent required to excel at any level of the sport, it takes discipline to adhere to this type of routine. Talent, when combined with disciplined preparation, produces outstanding performances.

*D*iscipline yourself
and others
won't need to.

JOHN WOODEN
*Legendary UCLA Head Basketball Coach*

The disciplined athlete adheres to principles and practices that enhance his or her performance. Those may include diet, food and beverage consumption before and during an event, muscle stretching and building, and cardiovascular development to build the capacity and endurance of the heart and lungs.

# The effort is what counts in everything.

JOHN WOODEN
*Legendary UCLA Head Basketball Coach*

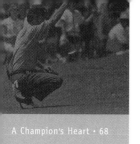

Athletes must go beyond the discipline of learning and excelling in practice and on the field. They must also learn to discipline their mind and body so as to adhere to the rules of the game or competition. Often it requires great discipline to learn and abide by those rules, especially in the heat of competition. That is when the mind and body want to succumb to shortcuts and outbursts of anger that are outside the boundaries of the game. Such failure can result in penalties and even defeat.

Athletes must have steadfast endurance in practice and in competition. They must show up for every practice, learn every play or routine, practice techniques and skills, and work hard over long periods of time. As spiritual athletes we must also be steadfast and disciplined. We must learn to live by God's principles and the plan He has laid out in the Bible. Throughout life we must be disciplined in seeking to understand God's plan and in living by the guidance He offers.

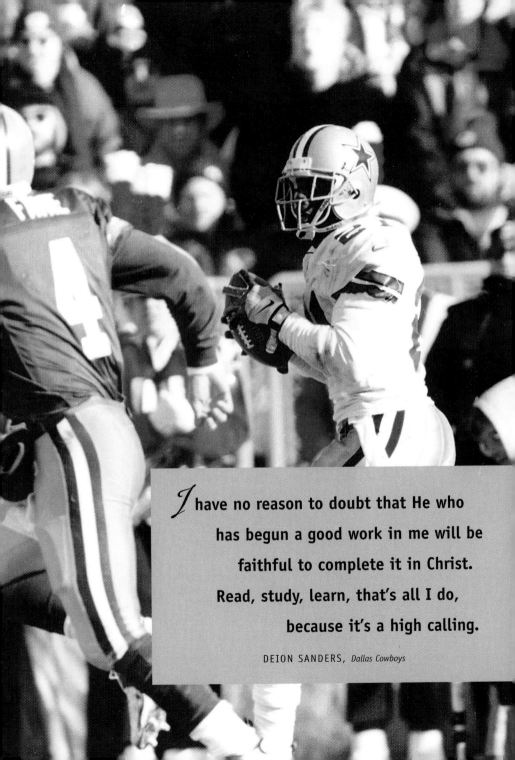

*I* have no reason to doubt that He who has begun a good work in me will be faithful to complete it in Christ. Read, study, learn, that's all I do, because it's a high calling.

DEION SANDERS, *Dallas Cowboys*

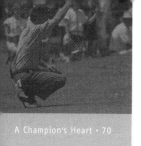

In this game of life, in the spiritual battlefield, and in the quest for meaning and purpose, there is good news for the spiritual athlete. We all get to play in the game. We not only get into the game—we are all winners with Christ! In his letter to the Hebrews, the apostle Paul puts it this way: *For we have become partakers of Christ if we hold the beginning of our confidence steadfast to the end* (Hebrews 3:14). However, as in athletics, there are Christians who do not have the discipline to regularly read the Bible, pray, and fellowship with other believers. In addition, they may not listen to the counsel God gives them directly through His word and through wise teachers, friends, and counselors.

The spiritual disciplines that I try to maintain
are roughly 20-30 minutes of prayer and/or
meditation twice a day (once in the morning
and once at about noon), a short time of
Scripture study before breakfast,
and a weekly Bible study with
two other individuals as well as
weekly worship at my church.

TOM OSBORNE
*Former Head Football Coach – University of Nebraska*

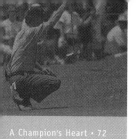

When we are disciplined to seek God on a regular basis, we have the opportunity to:

(1) find our potential in Him,

(2) recognize opportunities to serve Him,

(3) gain wisdom and knowledge, and

(4) bear fruit for His purposes.

*The* discipline, work, training, victories, and disappointments in life teach us some of our greatest lessons.

BOB BARDWELL
*Wheelchair Marthoner*

**POWER** point #6

A disciplined
life is the
mark of
a winner
and the
will of
God!

# Chapter 7 | Conditioned for Opportunity

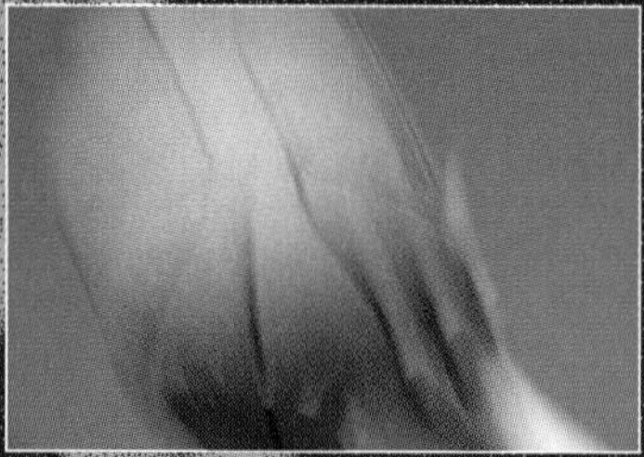

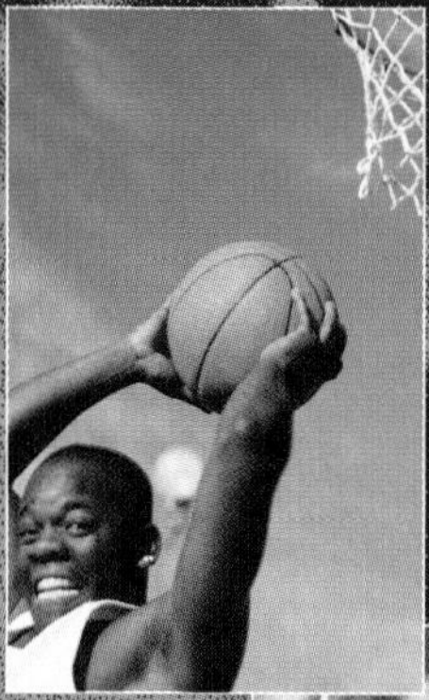

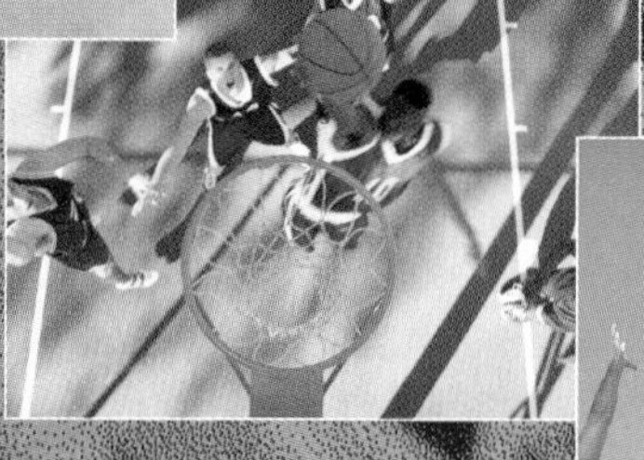

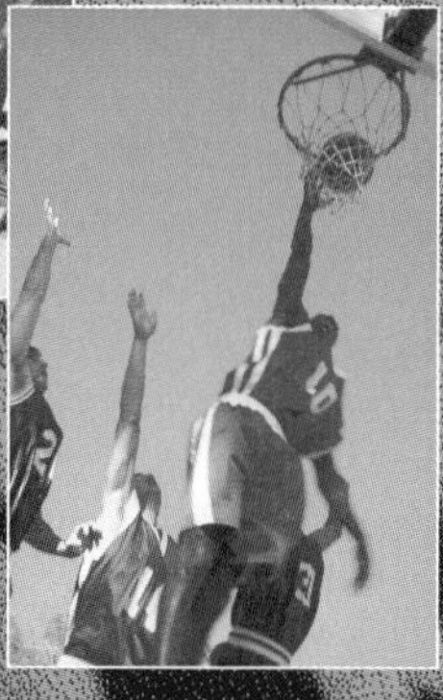

Blessed is the man who endures temptation; for when he has been approved, he will receive the crown of life which the Lord has promised to those who love Him.

JAMES 1:12

*W*ithout proper conditioning in all areas, you will fall short of your potential.

JOHN WOODEN
*Legendary UCLA Head Basketball Coach*

Conditioning is the **physical** preparation of the body, **mental** preparation of the brain, **emotional** preparation of the nervous system, and **spiritual** preparation of the heart. Even the most highly talented athlete is only as good as his or her physical, mental, emotional, and spiritual conditioning. Therefore, it is imperative that athletes work to become conditioned and to maintain that level of "fitness" in all four areas.

In athletic events there are always unknown variables that cannot be anticipated. These may be unforeseen opportunities to be captured or obstacles to overcome. Conditioned athletes are more likely to succeed in either case. In fact, preparation and conditioning will help athletes take advantage of those situations. By being well prepared for whatever may happen, they are able to take advantage of opportunities or overcome obstacles when they occur. King Solomon describes this in Ecclesiastes:

*The race is not to the swift, nor the battle to the strong, nor bread to the wise, nor riches to men of understanding, nor favor to men of skill; but time and chance happen to them all.*

ECCLESIASTES 9:11

This "chance" in the Hebrew language means "a casual occurrence." It is an opportunity, sometimes disguised as an obstacle, that occurs in our midst. Given that some "chances" will surely occur, it is wise for each of us to be prepared (conditioned) to handle them effectively.

# $\mathcal{B}$e ready. Be ready. The time will come.

SHERRI COALE
*Oklahoma Sooners Women's Basketball Coach*

God has created us in a wonderfully complex way. He created us in His own image. To operate effectively and utilize what He has created in us, we must be physically, mentally, emotionally, and spiritually conditioned. While we are not all equally talented, we can each condition ourselves to be prepared to meet the demands placed on the course of our lives. Each of us has been given talents and abilities along with spiritual gifts that make us unique. We must learn to understand our personal uniqueness and how God wants to use our capabilities for His Kingdom.

*There are diversities of gifts, but the same Spirit.*

*There are differences of ministries, but the same Lord.*

*And there are diversities of activities,*

*but it is the same God who works all in all.*

*But the manifestation of the Spirit is given*

*to each one for the profit of all.*

1 CORINTHIANS 12:4-7

The process of conditioning and learning to face these demands is a lifelong process. It begins in the home as our parents teach us, challenge us, and foster our growth. It continues in the educational system and on into vocational training or college. Our "conditioning" continues as we work for a living and identify a career. It does not end there because we are students throughout life. We must learn to adapt and deal with the information and opportunities that come along. Part of our conditioning for these opportunities is in the way we prepare our mind, emotions, and body to acquire and adapt new information and new skills. Life is, in part, a process of learning to learn.

God does not operate at random or without design and timing. However, throughout our lives He allows us many opportunities to respond to the events that occur around us. We can overcome, rather than simply live with, the circumstances we face. God expects His children to respond to the opportunities He puts in their path. He expects us to act on and take advantage of these opportunities in ways that are consistent with His word, precepts, and principles. In so doing, we bring glory to Him and serve His kingdom here on earth.

*The* **Christian life is not an instantaneous conquering. It's a process of becoming.**

GARY SCOTT
*Mountain Climber who challenged
Mount Everest alone*

At our place of work we cannot predict every opportunity or obstacle we will face in the course of a day or week. We certainly cannot predict every step of our career. The person who is conditioned and prepared is able to seize those opportunities and overcome the obstacles. Even if we do not have the skills to handle the new situation, by learning to be problem solvers and overcomers we are better prepared.

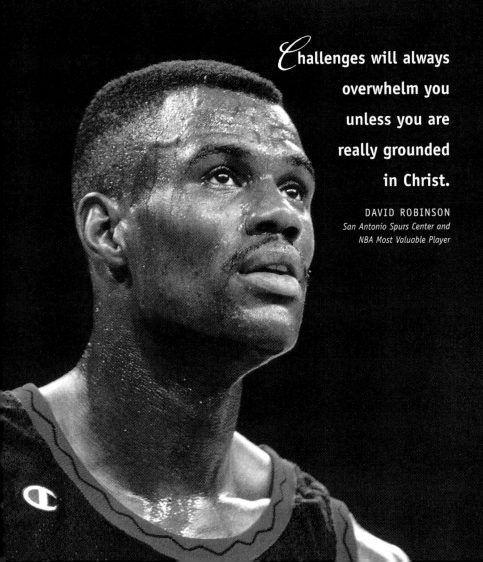

*C*hallenges will always overwhelm you unless you are really grounded in Christ.

DAVID ROBINSON
*San Antonio Spurs Center and*
*NBA Most Valuable Player*

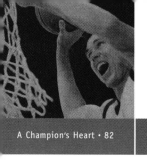

# CREATE OPPORTUNITIES

Some people say they're doing pretty well "under the circumstances." Spiritual athletes "get out from under the circumstances"—by preparation and conditioning to "create opportunities" for themselves, others, and God.

# DAILY CONDITIONING

*He* doesn't even stand up first.
He rolls out of bed and he
goes on his knees and he prays.
He makes that decision every day,
to humble himself in prayer.

FELICITY CUNNINGHAM
*commenting on her husband, Randall Cunningham,*
*Vikings Quarterback*

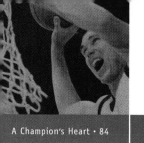

# PRAY FOR OPPORTUNITIES

*I* believe there is power in prayer

and it does make a difference in our lives.

I spend time praying the morning of every game.

During this time, I pray for each player

on our football team who will be playing.

I pray for their safety and that they

make the most of their God-given talents.

We also pray for our opponents

at our chapel services.

They are an important part of the game,

and we hope that the actions of

players on both sides will honor Him.

TOM OSBORNE

POWER
point #7

**Conditioning prepares our knuckles for knocking on the door of opportunity.**

Rejoicing
in hope,
patient
in tribulation,
continuing
steadfastly
in prayer.

ROMANS 12:12

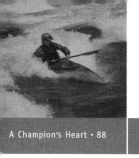

# PREPARATION

Outstanding athletes are known for their grit, tenacity, and unwillingness to give up. They are strong even when it appears that defeat is inevitable. We often see football games where one team is behind by two touchdowns or basketball games where a team is down by a wide margin with a minute or two left. Even if nearly all the fans have left their seats, and the television sets have been switched to another channel, the coach, captain, or quarterback may call several time outs to save time and discuss the strategy. Despite the obstacle, they have prepared for such a situation and seek to overcome the odds and pull out a win. The better teams and players will not give up despite the challenge of this situation. In his book, *Winning Every Day: The Game Plan for Success*, Coach Lou Holtz writes: "I have always told my players that I can forgive physical mistakes. Missed tackles, missed passes, missed plays . . . they're all part of the game. But poor preparation is intolerable, no matter what profession you are in."

Adversity comes in many forms. It may be the overwhelming odds we face, injury or loss of players, or "off" performances by a star of the team. It may come in the form of what appear to be bad calls by umpires or referees, or unrealistic marks by judges. It may come from weather or field conditions, a bad bounce, or an unfortunate judgment by an official. Preparing for such adversity can only come by conditioning to handle even the unexpected. In addition to these forms of adversity, preparation includes learning to handle our internal emotions in the wide variety of situations that can occur . . . even those that may seem totally unfair.

*A*dversity can make us better.
We must be challenged
to improve,
and adversity is
the challenger.

JOHN WOODEN
*Legendary UCLA Head Basketball Coach*

*And let us not grow weary while doing good,*
*for in due season we shall reap*
*if we do not lose heart.*

GALATIANS 6:9

*T*ake four letters out of the middle of . . .
**DON'T QUIT! . . .**
**and you have an admonition for life . . . DO IT!**

Knowing there will be adversity, and having the power to
overcome the obstacles, is the mark of a champion. Champions
may not win every time, but they never quit in the middle of
the event, game, round, series, or season.

*If* you walk with God, you can have victory,

even when things get really tough.

So the challenge is to walk with God.

DAVID ROBINSON

Do Christians lose battles in life? Yes! Are we losers or failures? No, not if we refuse to give up or quit. If we have faith, true faith in the One who came to save us from the ultimate defeat, then we can never be a failure. A failure is one who accepts a defeat as a final resting place instead of building upon a setback as a basis for future success. We become losers only when we accept defeat as the norm for our life and quit trying. Instead, we need to see momentary defeat or failure as an opportunity to learn and improve.

Momentary defeat is opportunity to move forward toward the final victory.

Jesus told His followers they *"always ought to pray and not lose heart"* (Luke 18:1).

*Adversity* often produces the unexpected opportunity.

Look for it. Appreciate and utilize it.

JOHN WOODEN

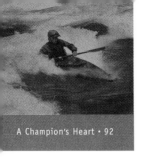

Spiritual athletes all always prepared for a comeback. No matter how badly they get beat one day, they re-group to prepare themselves for a comeback. If the first half has been a disaster, it is the heart of a winner who believes a comeback is possible. Always believe there is still hope.

## $\mathscr{L}$ife is more manageable when I realize it calls for one comeback after another.

DAVE DRAVECKY

Successful athletes do not dwell on their losses or mistakes. They deal with the problem or weakness (physical, mental, emotional or spiritual) that led to the mistake, loss, or failure. Then, they press on toward the next goal and level of achievement. This concept is found in Isaiah 43:25 and Hebrews 8:12 and 10:17, which can be summarized: God does not hold our past mistakes or failures against us; neither should we.

We must also resist Satan's efforts to bog us down with our past mistakes or shortcomings. We need only repent of them, seek forgiveness, make restitution (when appropriate), and learn from the situation.

*My little children, these things I write to you,*
*so that you may not sin.*
*And if anyone sins,*
*we have an Advocate with the Father,*
*Jesus Christ the righteous.*

*And He Himself is the propitiation*
*for our sins,*
*and not for ours only*
*but also for the whole world.*

1 JOHN 2:1-2

After facing the attack of the enemy and enlisting the protection and firepower of the living God, prepare for a comeback, and move onward and upward to victory. We need to be reminded that Jesus and His Word is the only preparation we need for the spiritual battle against the enemy, Satan, who seeks to spoil the victory that we have attained in Christ.

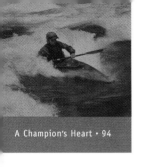

*It is Christ who died,*
*and furthermore is also risen,*
*who is even at the right hand of God,*
*who also makes intercession for us.*
*Who shall separate us from the love of Christ?*
*Shall tribulation, or distress,*
*or persecution, or famine,*
*or nakedness, or peril, or sword?*
*As it is written:*
*"For Your sake we are killed all day long;*
*We are accounted as sheep*
*for the slaughter."*
*Yet in all these things we are*
*more than conquerors*
*through Him who loved us.*

ROMANS 8:34-37

**Anything can happen at any given point in time.**

**You've just got to deal with it.**

**—You get over it and go on down the road.**

**That's what we do.**

BILL ELLIOTT
*NASCAR Driver*

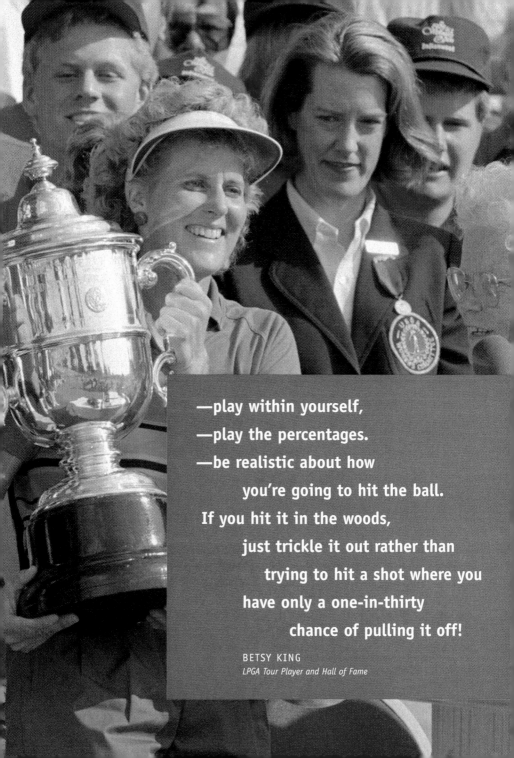

—play within yourself,
—play the percentages.
—be realistic about how
    you're going to hit the ball.
If you hit it in the woods,
        just trickle it out rather than
            trying to hit a shot where you
        have only a one-in-thirty
            chance of pulling it off!

BETSY KING
*LPGA Tour Player and Hall of Fame*

*B*eing a Christian
doesn't eliminate all
the problems in your life,
but the Lord is your strength
and Jesus will help you
solve the problems.

ALLEN BACH
*World Champion Rodeo Team Roper*

*O*nce the opportunity arrives,
it's too late to prepare.

JOHN WOODEN

# POWER
## point #8

When we prepare
ourselves
for adversity,
our setbacks and
losses become
building blocks
rather than
stumbling blocks
and stepping stones
instead of
headstones.

Chapter 9 | **Devoted to Sacrifice**

For whoever
desires to
save his life
will lose it,
but whoever
loses his life
for My sake
will save it.

LUKE 9:24

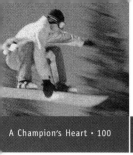

# SACRIFICE IS VITAL

Dedicated athletes are willing to undergo whatever it takes to achieve victory or just simply to do their very best. They willingly pay the price of sacrifice every day, in season and out. The very best have the internal fortitude to push themselves beyond the levels others are willing to attempt. Often this involves playing with discomfort, pain, or injury. To the very best athletes, their willingness to suffer exceeds their need for comfort. They will stand in the gap where they are needed. Coach Lou Holtz explained the importance of sacrifice when he wrote: "You may be asking why I think sacrifice is vital to any winning game plan. My answer is simple: So few people are willing to make them. Those of you who habitually do that little bit extra will enjoy a tremendous edge over your competition."

At times athletes have to suffer the humiliation of a poor performance. At times they must accept the criticism or misunderstanding of a misinformed audience. During a critical game with Green Bay near the end of the 1997 season, Brad Johnson, the Viking quarterback, dropped the ball several times in the motion of passing. At the time the announcers and fans criticized him without realizing that Brad had damage to a vertebra in his neck

and would require a delicate and painful operation on the spinal column. The effect of this damage to that particular vertebra is the loss of feeling and strength in the hand. Brad had to suffer not only the pain of this condition, the subsequent operation and recovery, but also the humiliation of the fans and announcers.

Every athlete knows the meaning of the phrase, "No pain, no gain." Athletes must sacrifice in order to be as good as their abilities will allow. They have to endure the pain of workouts, practice, and the game itself. It takes strain to train. The body may hurt from training, extended use of certain muscles, and the pounding of practice and game conditions. Furthermore, for all the pluses that come from athletic endeavors, the participants must often give up part of their social or recreational time. They must work hard to find time for academic pursuits or personal interests.

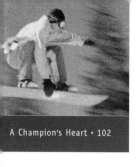

Christ made the ultimate sacrifice for us on the cross. Our life of faith involves being a living sacrifice to God. We are to see our life, work, ministry, and all that we do, as being done unto the Lord. We should willingly pay the price to make all our actions and thoughts honorable to Him. We must seek to make our life all that God intended. In so doing we are a living sacrifice to Him, our family, the Body of Christ, and the world — holy and acceptable to God.

*I beseech you therefore, brethren, by the mercies of God, that you present your bodies a living sacrifice, holy, acceptable to God, which is your reasonable service.*

ROMANS 12:1

$\mathcal{M}$y mom told me that this jet-ski thing

was not impressive to her and that

if my grades dropped she'd put a stop to it.

So between practice sessions I'd be

studying chemistry or some crazy thing.

I found out that God stretches you.

He stretches your faith. You work hard,

and He's pleased with your perseverance.

I worked very hard, and kept the grades up.

CHRISTY CARLSON
*Six-Time National Champion and Five-Time World Champion Jet-Ski Racer*

Sadly, too many people, both believers and non-believers, seem to think that their life does not count for much. Quite to the contrary, every individual needs to recognize that God put him or her on earth to make a difference, to count for something. As followers of Christ we are to sacrifice, just as He has sacrificed for us, so that we may participate in His victory. Sacrifice means giving up part of our own identity, success, and pleasure in order to experience significance and meaning in life.

## SACRIFICES FOR OTHERS

*If* you want to be a team player, there are sacrifices to make. By no means am I comparing my sacrifices to the sacrifice that Christ made for us, but that's just a small picture of pretty much the same thing. I have to make sacrifices day in and day out for the betterment of the team, as He made sacrifices for the betterment of the world—for those who want to follow him.

HOWARD GRIFFITH
*Fullback for the Denver Broncos*
*Lead Blocker Paving the Way for Terrell Davis*

## SACRIFICE COMES FROM THE HEART

*Y*ou can do all kinds of nice things for people.

But if you don't have love in your heart,

if you're not serving God, it means nothing.

DAVID ROBINSON

*G*ather My saints together to Me,

'those who have made a covenant

with Me by sacrifice.

PSALM 50:5

God takes no pleasure in our losses. He does not want to see us beaten down in life. Winning and success are neither sinful nor contrary to God's ways. God expects us, as His children, to be overcomers and to achieve His will on earth. Winning and success will come in various forms and at different levels for each individual. However, ultimate significance for everyone occurs through sacrifice of our life to Him. In this way, it is like athletics and all of life — sacrifice is required for success.

*For as many as are led by the Spirit of God,*
*these are sons of God. For you did not receive*
*the spirit of bondage again to fear,*
*but you received the Spirit of adoption by whom*
*we cry out, "Abba, Father." The Spirit Himself*
*bears witness with our spirit that we are children of God,*
*and if children, then heirs—heirs of God and*
*joint heirs with Christ, if indeed we suffer with Him,*
*that we may also be glorified together.*

ROMANS 8:14-17

# God Teaches Us Through Experience

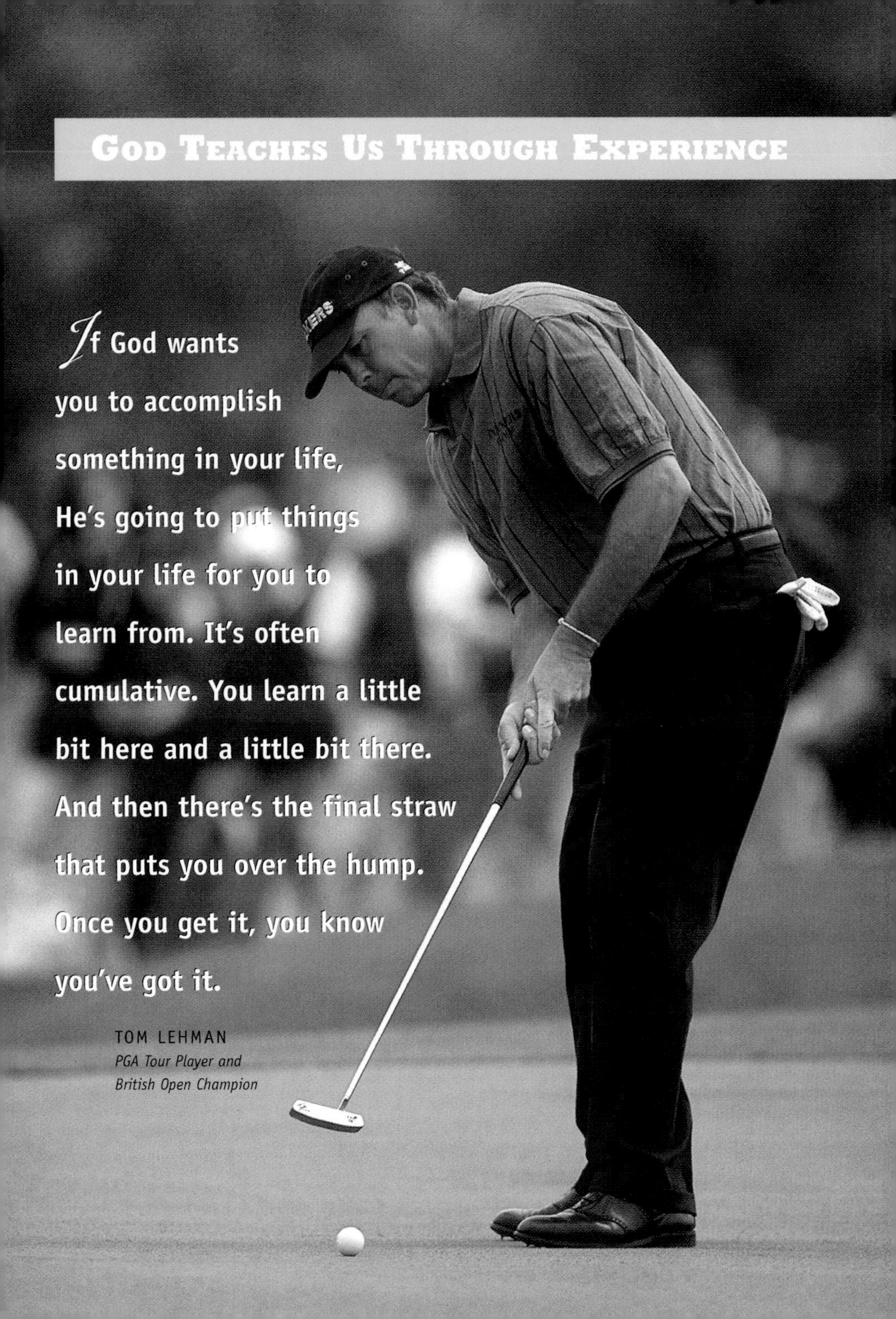

If God wants you to accomplish something in your life, He's going to put things in your life for you to learn from. It's often cumulative. You learn a little bit here and a little bit there. And then there's the final straw that puts you over the hump. Once you get it, you know you've got it.

TOM LEHMAN
*PGA Tour Player and British Open Champion*

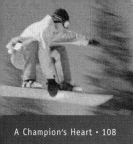

*We . . . glory in tribulations, knowing that tribulation produces perseverance; and perseverance, character; and character, hope.*

ROMANS 5:3-4

When I came to see the big picture

—that it's God who gave me the talent to play

—then I developed a whole new perspective

on the game and on life.

God demands the very best I can be for Him.

At the same time, He's the One who

gives me the strength to be just that!

RYAN WALTER
*Center for the NHL Vancouver Canucks*

POWER point #9

Sacrifice without love is void of meaning. Love without sacrifice is void of commitment. Christ's sacrifice demonstrated His love for us. Our love for Him is demonstrated in our sacrifice for others.

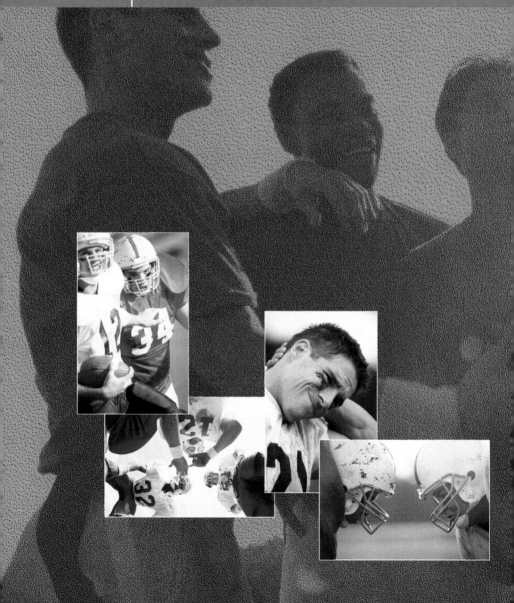

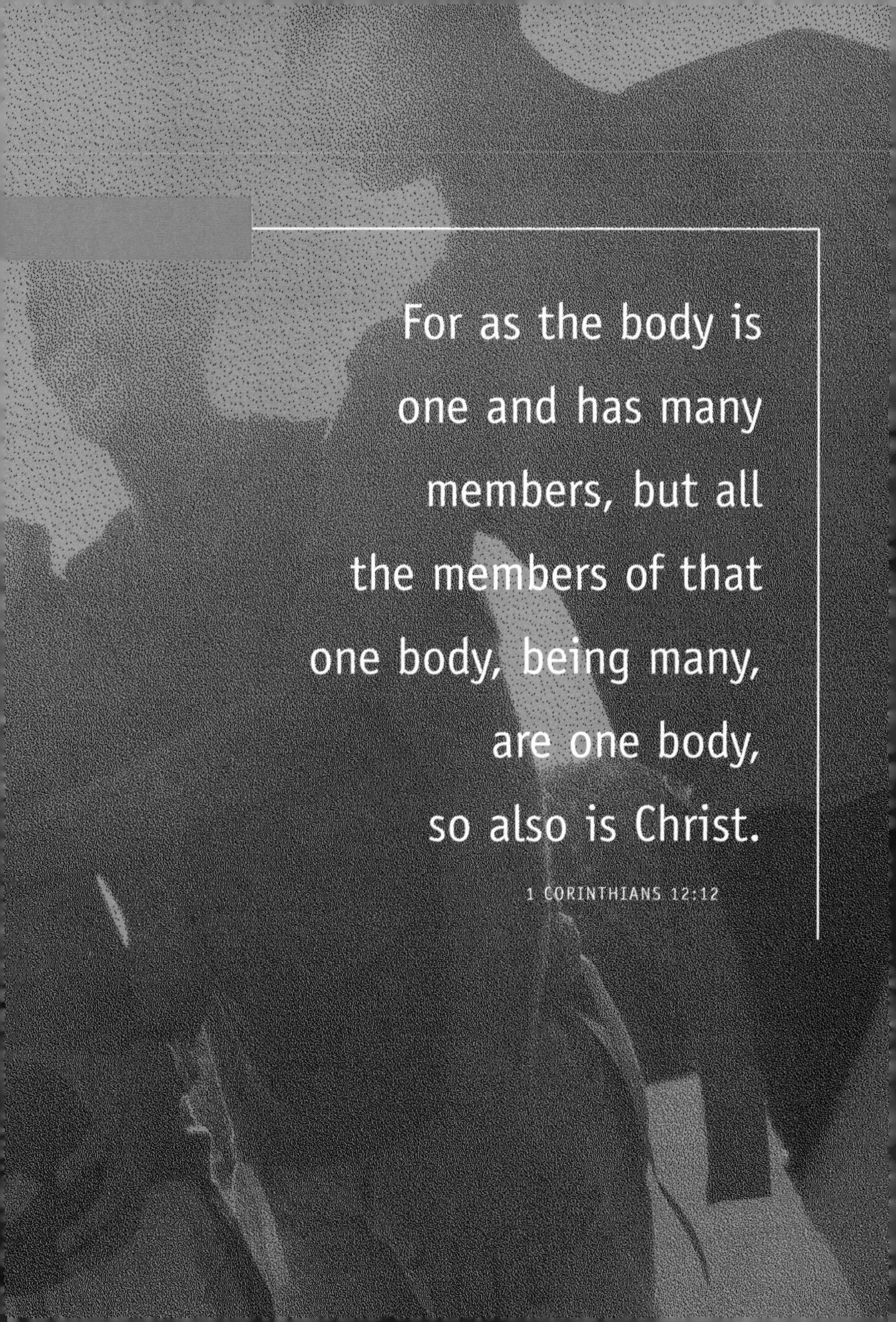

For as the body is
one and has many
members, but all
the members of that
one body, being many,
are one body,
so also is Christ.

1 CORINTHIANS 12:12

# THERE IS TEAMWORK IN NEARLY EVERYTHING WE DO.

It is almost always a part of athletics. The success of the team reflects the cooperative effort of the individuals. Success is more than the sum of the individual performances of the players. It is the synergistic effect of their working together for a common goal. Each team member must be focused on the overall team goal as well as fulfilling his or her own role for the team.

*U*nderstanding that the good of the group comes first is fundamental to being a highly productive member of a team.

JOHN WOODEN
*Legendary UCLA Head Basketball Coach*

# TEAM SPIRIT

Even when we participate in an event on our own, we may be a part of a team. Furthermore, we are almost always involved with a coach or trainer who is, in effect, our teammate. The athlete may be helped by a sports psychologist and a conditioning coach. This is certainly true in sports like gymnastics, track, skiing, tennis, and golf where the athlete performs in an event alone, but receives ongoing coaching and encouragement in order to perfect his or her conditioning and technique. Finally, with technology playing such a key part in the equipment for many sports, the representatives of these specialized pieces of equipment can become a partner. They may help identify just the right equipment for a particular athlete's style, strengths, and limitations. The proper bat, skis, racket, clubs, mitt, bobsled, or snowboard can make a big difference if it is well suited to us.

*It* means being not just willing
but eager to sacrifice
personal interest or glory
for the welfare of all.

JOHN WOODEN

*I* just tell God,
"Use me how you will.
My life belongs to you."

RANDALL CUNNINGHAM
*Vikings Pro-Bowl Quarterback*

When we each serve in the capacities for which we are best suited and gifted by God, we not only serve Christ, but we also serve one another. By learning how God has uniquely prepared each of us to serve Him and His body, we function effectively as a team. We are able to meet the needs of one another and to reach out to those who are not yet believers in Christ. We have an offensive role in winning others to Him. We must also mount a defensive strategy in Jesus' name against Satan who seeks to destroy or diminish our impact.

*N* ow that I'm older and I see the younger guys
and the mistakes that they're making,
it makes you wish that you could tell them
and show them which direction they're going in.

JAKE BARNES
*World Champion Rodeo Team Roper*

The Christian faith is both an individual and a team event. As individuals, we are each responsible for our own steps of faith. No one can get us into heaven. We can only get there based on our own personal faith in Jesus Christ. We are also responsible for living our own life in accordance with God's expectations as defined in the Bible.

However, Christianity is also a team event. Collectively, Christians are the body of Christ on earth. We cannot and do not live our life of faith in a vacuum apart from others. Our teammates in the Christian life are the body of believers in Christ, especially those with whom we fellowship on a regular basis. We function together to bring about His will here on earth. We each have unique gifts and abilities with which we are to serve the body and Christ. No one individual has all the tools and talents needed to survive, let alone make a difference. We could not function alone as Christians and it would be a dreadfully difficult and lonely task if we tried to do so.

*A* life is not important

except in the impact

it has on others.

JACKIE ROBINSON
*Brooklyn Dodgers baseball player*
*in the 50's — First black player*
*in the Major Leagues*

By serving God in the way He has uniquely prepared each of us, we are able to fulfill His will. At the same time, we find personal fulfillment. We discover significance by utilizing the gifts and talents God has given each of us to serve Him. We do so by contributing to the team effort, submitting our own will to the will of the "Coach." We also subordinate our own short-term goals and desire for recognition in order to help achieve the team's goals.

*Every* activity and every relationship on earth
will fulfill its ultimate purpose only when
it drives me toward a vital,
growing relationship with him [God].

DAVE DRAVECKY

The spiritual athlete, like the athlete in sports, is able to achieve significance through the success of the team. The spiritual athlete discovers meaning in life by committing to serve the Creator and the body of Christ, working together to meet God's mission here on earth and eternally in heaven. We discover the worth that God has built into us when we open our heart up to His truth and influence in our life.

*for as the body is one and has many members,*
 *but all the members of that one body,*
 *being many, are one body, so also is Christ.*

1 CORINTHIANS 12:12

In any team effort each individual needs to do his or her part. Each person must be motivated and committed to the effort. When this occurs it is possible to produce an effort that is more than the simple sum of the parts. There is a potential for synergy that produces more than was ever possible by looking at the talents of the individuals on the team. This requires each individual to be focused on the team instead of self.

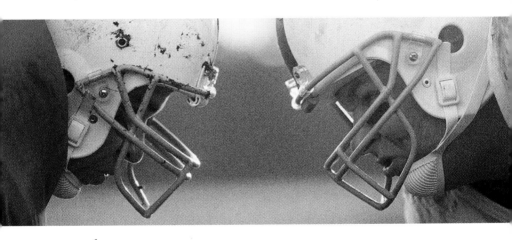

*If one member suffers, all the members suffer with it;*
 *or if one member is honored,*
 *all the members rejoice with it.*
 *Now you are the body of Christ,*
 *and members individually.*

1 CORINTHIANS 12:25-27

One aspect of teamwork is accountability to one another. In athletics there are often those who encourage us to do the right things to prepare ourselves. Training partners and coaches may be there to hold us accountable for our preparation and follow through. They may help us to be strong and resist temptation to quit or slack off on practice, proper diet, and avoidance of drugs and alcohol.

*If* I'm able to draw people to the Lord,
then they'll have that joy and that love for Him.
The fame and the money and the rankings
can't compare to touching people's lives
and encouraging them in the Lord,
because that's something that
lasts a lifetime and beyond.

MICHAEL CHANG
*Professional Tennis Player*

# POWER point #10

The spiritual athlete is, above all else, a team player. He or she finds meaning and purpose in life by serving Jesus as a member of God's team.

# ACKNOWLEDGEMENTS

Grateful acknowledgments for quotations included in this book are made to the following:

Amstutz, Amber. "Meeting the Challenge," by Dean Jackson, *Sharing the Victory*. Fellowship of Christian Athletes.

Bach, Allen. Fellowship of Christian Cowboys, Inc., Colorado Springs, Colorado.

Barnes, Jake. Fellowship of Christian Cowboys, Inc., Colorado Springs, Colorado.

Bardwell, Bob. *The Marathons of Life*. Stewartville, MN: Bob and Jode Bardwell.

Burt, Adam. "His Own Story of Faith: Adam Burt," with Lois Thomson, taken from *Sports Spectrum*, a Christian sports magazine. Used by permission. Grand Rapids, MI, (November 1997, p. 27). For subscription information call 1-800-283-8333.

Carlson, Christy. "Speed Queen," by Amy Meyering, taken from *Sports Spectrum*, a Christian sports magazine. Used by permission. Grand Rapids, MI, (October 1997, p. 15). For subscription information call 1-800-283-8333.

Carter, Cris. "Four for the Show," by Troy Pearson, taken from *Sports Spectrum*, a Christian sports magazine. Used by permission. Grand Rapids, MI, (January/February 1999, p. 27). For subscription information call 1-800-283-8333.

Carter, Joe. "Spreading His Gift," by John Dodderidge, *Sharing the Victory*. Fellowship of Christian Athletes (May 1998).

Coale, Sherri. "Ready and Willing," by Robyne Baker, *Sharing the Victory*. Fellowship of Christian Athletes (February 1999).

Chang, Michael. "The Chang Gang," by Christin Ditchfield, taken from *Sports Spectrum*, a Christian sports magazine. Used by permission. Grand Rapids, MI, (June1998, p. 11). For subscription information call 1-800-283-8333.

Cunningham, Felicity. *Minneapolis Star and Tribune* (December 25, 1998, C1).

Cunningham, Randall. *Minneapolis Star and Tribune* (December 25, 1998, C1, C6).

Custer, Cody Mark. Fellowship of Christian Cowboys, Inc., Colorado Springs, Colorado.

Darden, Robert and P.J. Richardson. *The Way of an Eagle*. Nashville, TN: Thomas Nelson Publishers, 1996. (Betsy King, p.97; Tom Lehman, p.127; Barb Mucha, p.163; Loren Roberts, p.201; DeWitt Weaver, p.255)

Dravecky, Dave with Connie Neal. Taken from *The Worth of a Man*. Grand Rapids, MI: Zondervan Publishing House, Copyright ©1996 by David F. Dravecky. Used by permission of Zondervan Publishing House.

Eagles, Mike. "Capital Punishment," by Jeff Gilbert, taken from *Sports Spectrum*, a Christian sports magazine. Used by permission. Grand Rapids, MI, (February 1996, p. 29). For subscription information call 1-800-283-8333.

Elliott, Bill. *1995 Indianapolis Stock Cars Yearbook*, by Carl Hungness, Speedway, Indiana.

Frost, Scott. "Overcoming any Obstacle" by Arthur L. Lindsay, *Sharing the Victory*, Fellowship of Christian Athletes (February 1998).

Gordon, Jeff. *Winston Cup Illustrated* . Street and Smith's Sports Group, Charlotte, NC. (August 1998).

Green, A.C. quote taken from "Against the Flow" by Dave Branon, taken from *Slam Dunk: Winning Players Talk about Basketball, Family, and Faith*. Copyright 1994, Moody Bible Institute of Chicago. Moody Press. Used by permission.

Griffith, Howard. "Blocking Bronco," by Allen Palmeri, taken from *Sports Spectrum*, a Christian sports magazine. Used by permission. Grand Rapids, MI, (January/February 1999, p. 28). For subscription information call 1-800-283-8333.

Harris, Gerald. *Olympic Heroes: World-Class Athletes Winning at Life*. Nashville, TN: Broadman & Holman Publishers, 1996.

Holtz, Lou. *Winning Every Day: The Game Plan for Success.* New York: Harper Business, A Division of Harper Collins Publishers, 1998.

Irving, Julius ("Dr. J"). "The Good Doctor" by Dave Branon, taken from *Slam Dunk: Winning Players Talk about Basketball, Family, and Faith.* Copyright 1994, Moody Bible Institute of Chicago. Moody Press. Used by permission.

Janaszak, Steve. Quote on pg. 24 taken from *Winning the Face-Off of Life* ©1992 by International Bible Society all rights reserved.

Jarvis, Doug. Quote on pg. 36 taken from *Winning the Face-Off of Life* ©1992 by International Bible Society all rights reserved.

Johnson, Dave with Verne Becker. *Aim High: An Olympic Decathlete's Inspiring Story.* Grand Rapids, MI: Zondervan Publishing House. Copyright ©1994 by Dave Johnson. Used by permission of Zondervan Publishing House.

Landry, Tom with Gregg Lewis. Taken from *Tom Landry: An Autobiography*, Grand Rapids, MI: Zondervan Publishing House. Copyright ©1990 by Tom Landry. Used by permission of Zondervan Publishing House.

Martin, Mark. *Winston Cup Illustrated*, Street and Smith's Sports Group, Charlotte, NC (September, 1997).

Osborne, Tom. "Tom Osborne: A Spiritual Legacy," Interview by Gordon Thiessen, *Sharing the Victory*, Fellowship of Christian Athletes, (February 1998).

Osborne, Tom. "Strong to the Finish," *Sharing the Victory*, Fellowship of Christian Athletes (February 1998).

Perez, Tony. "Winning Attitude," by Robyne Baker, *Sharing the Victory*, Fellowship of Christian Athletes (February 1999).

Retton, Mary Lou. "Cool Under Pressure" in *Olympic Heroes: World-Class Athletes Winning at Life* by Gerald Harris, Nashville, TN: Broadman & Holman Publishers, 1996. Used by permission.

Robinson, David. Taken from *How to Raise An MVP*, by Ambrose and Freda Robinson. Grand Rapids, MI: Zondervan Publishing House. Copyright ©1996 by Ambrose and Freda Robinson. Used by permission of Zondervan Publishing House.

Robinson, David. "It All Adds Up to Greatness," by Dave Branon, taken from *Slam Dunk: Winning Players Talk about Basketball, Family, and Faith.* Copyright 1994, Moody Bible Institute of Chicago. Moody Press. Used by permission.

Ruettger, Ken with Dave Branon. *Home Field Advantage: A Dad's Guide to the Power of Role Modeling,* Sisters, Oregon: Multnomah Books, 1995.

Sanders Deion. *Power, Money, & Sex: How Success Almost Ruined My Life*, Nashville, TN: Word Publishing, 1998.

Scott, Gary. "Peril on Everest," by Gary Scott with W. Terry Whalin, *Sports Spectrum*, (May 1998).

Sheard, Jim and Wally Armstron  g. *In His Grip: Foundations for Life and Golf*, Nashville: J Countryman Division of Word Publishing, 1997.

Singletary, Mike. "A Middle Line-Backer Defends the Family," by Jennie Chandler, *Sharing the Victory*, (February, 1999).

Smith, Charlotte. "Facing Adversity: Charlotte Smith Leans on God During Tough Times after Leaving College," by John Dodderidge, *Sharing the Victory* (January 1998).

Taffarel, Claudio. "Taffarael Live!," taken from *Sports Spectrum*, a Christian sports magazine. Used by permission. Grand Rapids, MI, (June 1998). For subscription information call 1-800-283-8333.

Walter, Ryan. Quote on pg. 103 taken from *Winning the Face-Off of Life* ©1992 by International Bible Society all rights reserved.

Waltrip, Darrell. *Winston Cup Illustrated*, Charlotte, NC: Street and Smith's Sports Group,. (December 1997).

White, Reggie. "End Game," Interview with Roman Gabriel III, *Sports Spectrum*, (January-February 1999).

White, Reggie. ESPN Interview by Roy Firestone on Easter Sunday, 1993.

Wooden, John with Steve Jamison. Reprinted from *Wooden: A Lifetime of Observations and Reflections On and Off the Court.* Lincolnwood, IL: Contemporary Books, ©1997. Used with permission of NTC/Contemporary Publishing Group, Inc.

Wooden, John. Reprinted from *They Call Me Coach*, Chicago: Contemporary Books, ©1988. Used with permission of NTC/Contemporary Publishing Group, Inc.

## THE WINNER'S CREED

*S*trive for excellence in thought, word, and deed.

Acknowledge the Almighty in all that you do.

Love your friends, speak the truth, practice fidelity

and honor your father and mother.

These godly principles are the foundation of life.

They make you strong of character,

give you hope, and put you on

the path of significance.

JOHN PETERSON